God Bless
you always.

Rebecca
Christmas 2011
Love
Grandma
& Grandpa

To: Rebecca Mazuryk.

From: Grandpa & Grandma M.
Christmas 2010

You are our #1 granddaughter
& you are Truly amazing.
Love you
so much.
forever.

Also by Ashley Rice

girls rule
Love Is Me and You
Thanks for Being My Friend
You Go, Girl... Keep Dreaming

Library of Congress Control Number: 2005905356
ISBN: 978-1-59842-066-1

Certain trademarks are used under license.
BLUE MOUNTAIN PRESS is registered in U.S. Patent and Trademark Office.

Printed in China.
Second Printing: 2008

Blue Mountain Arts, Inc.
P.O. Box 4549, Boulder, Colorado 80306

You Are

an Amazing Girl

...a very special book
about being you
and making your dreams
come true

Ashley Rice

Blue Mountain Press ™
Boulder, Colorado

Introduction

You Are an Amazing Girl is about a lot of things. It's about knowing how to win as well as how to lose and not get discouraged. It's about seeking out positive relationships in your life and not feeling pressured to be someone you're not. It's about expanding your mind and taking care of your body. It's about daring to take chances and making a contribution to the world with your talent. It's about caring and sharing and never giving up even when things get hard. But mostly it's about you — yes, you — and everything you can be.

You are an amazing girl
with style and courage.
You are an amazing girl
with big dreams and
lots of things to do.
You are an amazing girl...
...and this book is for you!

You are an amazing girl!

Being amazing can mean...

being **brave**
being athletic
being **intelligent**
being fabulous
being super
being funny...

...but mostly it means
being you...

...and the combination of traits,
talents and personal
qualities that make you who
you are!

You:

The **words** you *say*... ⭐

the **friends** you *make*... 😊

the **stuff** you *know*... ꩜

the **risks** you *take*... ♥ ꩜⭐

the **way** you *deal* with **things**... ☀

and the **life** *you make every* **day**...

(These
are all 😊
parts of what
make you so
great.)

It Takes Guts

It takes guts to dream
big dreams.
It takes guts to be who
you are.
It takes guts to see big
things: to learn, to grow, and —
knowing what you know —
to move forward in the direction
of your dreams.
It takes guts to dream these dreams.
It takes guts to stay who you are.

"Guts," of course, is just another name for courage. And without it we would never reach the stars.

Girl, you've got guts.

What Makes You Different?

You are **unique**, it's true...
There is no one else quite
like yOu. So don't hesitate
to step out from the
crowd, to show your own
style, your own smile,
your own way of doing
things...

Individuality is one of the greatest gifts in life.

Things You Should Know:

1. It's impossible to be perfect all the time and it's okay to make mistakes — they're part of what helps you learn, and they make you who you are.

2. In part, at least, you make your own luck: the more doors you try, the more doors or opportunities will open up for you and the more chances will come your way...

and...

3. (most importantly)...
   you're doing an
   awesome job!

If you are not sure
which way to go...
Ask your heart —
your heart will know.
When your mind
does not know what to say...
Your heart will ?
find a way...

➡

When you can't see
the finish line
or when your dreams
seem hard to find...

Know that you
know the way:
your heart will
lead you there
one day.

There's No Telling What You Can Do!

There's no telling what you can
   do if you don't get
   discouraged.
Concentrate on learning...
concentrate on courage.
Try a different way, or learn a
little more. Set goals and then
stick with them. When you fall down,
get up again. Believe in what you
do and who you are...

...and you'll
   go far.

A list of your dreams, goals, and accomplishments: ♡

As You Go On in This World:

Set goals and
do everything you
can to make them real.
Do not be afraid to
reach for the impossible.
Do not be afraid to
try your hardest...

...do not be afraid to
be **yourself** and
to show the world
all you can be.

On Hope:

You gotta have hope
and you gotta keep trying
and you gotta keep believing
that everything you are striving
for and trying to do is worth
something... 🦋🦋
And you gotta have some heart
and you gotta have drive...
but mostly you gotta have hope...

24

...and hope comes from inside.

It's not about how well
you do...
it's about how hard
you try and what kind
of a person you are.
And there are many
things we go through;
and there are many
things we will triumph
over...

And there will be times
when you'll fall down.
But there will be more
times when you pull
through. ☺
And you will find
greatness in your life.
And you will keep getting
stronger every second
of it.

Things to Do When You're Feeling Blue:

1. Call a friend
2. Read a book
3. Take a walk
4. Play a pick-up game (of basketball, soccer, tennis, hockey, etc.) with someone
5. Call your grandmother
6. Write an overdue letter
7. ...or journal entry

8. Send an e-card to someone special

9. Find a poem you like

10. Go outside and sit under a tree

11. Talk to someone you have not talked to in a while

12. Make something new

When you're feeling blue...
just find something to do...
and soon you will feel grand.

Every experience you go through
will make you stronger. There
may be times along the way when
you feel alone. But you never
really are! There are always
friends to be made and new
adventures to discover. There
are friends and family members
who respect you for who you are...

Wherever you go...
you are loved.

On Positivity:

Having a positive attitude is everything. If you think you can do something, you will be able to complete the task or achieve your specific dreams or goals. Things may not always turn out exactly as you had expected, but with a little work and a little willpower and a lot of determination...

You can do anything!

A Poem About Daring and Trying

For everyone who wants
to sing... ♪♩♪ ♫

or everyone who wants
to dream... ♥

and everyone who wants
to spin... ☺

and everyone who wants
to win... ☀

for everyone who wants
to dare... ✦

and everyone who wants to
bring forth greatness
in their lives... ♥

Do it!
Go for it!

On Having the Courage to Admit Mistakes:

As you get older, facing up to the consequences of your actions is a big part of growing up. If you make a mistake, don't be afraid to tell someone or to ask for help or advice. This is the best way to learn from your actions...

...and to keep on growing
up strong.

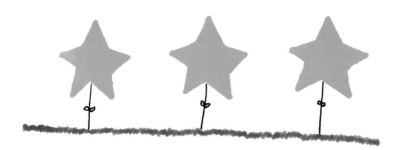

What If?

What would have happened if Amelia Earhart never got on a plane? What if Rosa Parks decided not to make a stand on that bus? What if Harriet Tubman had been too scared to pioneer the Underground Railroad, or if your favorite female novelist decided writing was too risky or too hard?

What if all these amazing women had decided not to step out from the crowd, decided not to take any chances? All of their achievements would be lost to us. Instead, they chose to give people hope and to fight for change.

What if you took a chance, gave it your all, stood up for something you believed in? There's no telling what you might do!

I believe!

power(ful) girls...

...workin' to | make their
goals and | dreams
come | true

You are one of the
power(ful) girls
I know.

♥ Other power(ful) girls you know ♥
or have heard about:

mommy
Puppy
Mrs. Turffyne
Daddy
Mrs. Ve

Stand Up Tall

Save the world for future generations.
You have the ability to change the world:
never fail to make a contribution.
Stand up. Stand tall. Speak up.
Always try your hardest...
Trust yourself.
Don't worry too much about the
little things...
Try to look at the long term...
Whatever you are doing, if you love it:
keep on trying...

Being an amazing girl
means you can make an amazing
contribution to the world...
(such as by being...)
an astronaut, a scientist,
a mathematician, an activist
an actress, a doctor,
an athlete, an artist...

What will you do? (The
possibilities are endless!)

On Facing the Competition:

These days, competition is fierce. It seems that there are more and more  talented people everywhere competing for the same place in the sun, the same patch of sky. However, there are three important things to remember when thinking about facing the competition.

The first thing is to forget the competition because — whatever you're doing — you are always, in the long run, really competing against yourself. In other words... it doesn't matter so much if you get 1st place or 3rd place. What really matters — in regards to what you believe you can do and what you have done in the past — is your own personal "time."

The second thing to remember when facing the competition is that everyone else feels pretty much the same way you do: Everyone else — though they may be competing against you in the actual race — is also trying to beat their own time.

Also (third): We can learn stuff from the people who are faster than us, and we can make friends with the people who run with us.

We can figure out ways to deal with our limitations in the process of competition, and thus find ways around those limitations. Competition often pushes us to work harder than we might work if we were left completely to our own devices.

No matter what you like to do or what goals you pursue, competition is a part of life and will most likely touch your life in some way.

Many have "failed" not from acting on their dreams, but by silencing their ideas due to a fear of the unknown — not acting at all.

From one dreamer to another: Don't give up.

"Rules"

Believe in **who** you are.

Make choices with your **brain**.

Make decisions with your **heart**. 💜

Define a finish line.

Finish what you **start**.

Make friends.

Stand tall.

Make **everything** you do worth doing.

A Poem About Rainbows

The road to any real change or accomplishment begins with a dream dreamed by one such as you. You may spend too long with your head in a book or a song in your head... but you look for the good and for rainbows in everything. You may believe too much. You may be a dreamer... and some people might say you should be more practical...

but practically every
idea — every act, big
or small — gets
its start from a
dream that begins
in the heart, like

a song.

(Always believe in your
amazing dreams.)

where you go

in this world is
up to you...

but the first thing to do
is to take care
of you.

Remember to take care of your body (you only get one!)... by cleaning in between your toes and behind your ears... by eating healthily and getting some exercise (whether it's running or ice-skating or dancing). Take care of your mind by expanding it through reading books... and take care of yourself in general!

Remember to surround yourself with healthy relationships. But what are healthy relationships exactly? Having healthy relationships means finding people who care about you, people who you respect and who respect you too. You should feel comfortable with your friends, and when you're with them you shouldn't feel pressured to do things you don't want to do...

Seeking out people you have things in common with is a good way to make friends. So is seeking out people who are different from you, because you can learn things from them and vice versa. Whether you are similar to or different from your best friends, the main thing is that you feel comfortable around them and don't feel pressured to be someone you're not.

Remember to...

Ask questions...

and get advice when you feel you need it...

Seek out people you admire — whether in books or in your own life — and try to learn from them...

Have fun with your interests and activities...

Give everything your best shot...

...and don't forget to
give yourself a pat
on the back every
once in a while —
you deserve it!

A star for you...

for all that you do...

...and all you are.

No matter where you go...

you are never far from your
goals...

And if life seems hard,

★ ★ ★ remember:
       ★

There are always great things

around you, surrounding you...

and great possibilities

ahead.

your future

Amazing girls are discoverers of new paths. Amazing girls are trailblazers and superheroines and confidantes. Amazing girls make their way with courage, strength, humor, and love. Amazing girls know how to laugh and to listen, to dare and to try. Amazing girls don't give up when the going gets tough.
Amazing girls...

are students and seekers, learners and keepers of goals and dreams and of the unexpected. Amazing girls believe in themselves and reach for the stars. Amazing girls are daughters and sisters and friends.

You are an amazing girl.

There is greatness within every girl...